How to Save Money Painlessly: Even When You Don't Have Any

By

PAUL STEPHENS

Table of Contents

Introduction

Are you the kind of person who has nothing left of their monthly salary when there is still a week left to the month? Do you struggle to make ends meet and in the process work yourself deeper into debt? It's stressful isn't it? I know all about that. I've been there. 'Been' being the operative word. I found a way out and so can you. There is hope and you can live differently. And you know what? It isn't in anyway less enjoyable. Quite the opposite. Looking at your savings increases and your debt disappear is a fantastic experience.

And all it takes to get there is a different mindset.

What's more, saving money is like training for other things. For once you've got the discipline and the attitude to change your finances you'll find that it's much easier to change other aspects of your life as well! Change begets change and before you know it, you'll be living your dream life, healthy, wealthy and happy. Sound too good to be true? You'll never know unless you try, do you? And even if it turns out I am wrong (which I'm not) you'll still be out of debt and saving money. So what's the worry?

But rather than me selling all the virtues of money management – after all, the fact that you picked up this book already shows that you're aware of them – let's dive straight in. Then you can judge for yourself whether this is the way forward! (Spoiler: It is).

Chapter 1: The Mindset and Principles of Money Management to Live By

Saving money is all about the right mindset. Yes, that might sound crazy. A mindset is, after all, an inner life thing while money most certainly is not. But that does not make it any less true. The reason it's internal it because it's all about how you choose to approach the problem. You can approach it either as a chore – something you hate doing, but have to – or you can look at it as an adventure, which is something you look forward to.

One of these activities is positive, the other negative. One of them is about seeing things in a way towards a better life, while the other is doings something you're supposed to do.

So make sure you have the right focus and mindset. What's that?

It Is About Saving, Not About Preventing Spending

You can look at it as being about moving away from something (spending) or moving towards something (savings). The difference might seem slight, but it is anything but. It's astronomical. You see, we're not very good at 'no' as a species. If I ask you not to think of a yellow dog with blue stripes, the first thing that pops into your mind is a rather odd looking dog. In the same way, if your goal is not to spend money, you'll constantly be thinking about the things you cannot buy.

And that will only serve to make it more likely that you'll go out and buy something.

And so, you have to change the mindset. To do that you need to find something to replace your desire to spend. Saving money is just as much about finding other ways to spend and occupy your time that are cheap and enjoyable as about not occupying your time with activities that are expensive. Otherwise you'll be bored stiff and, ironically, the only way out of that boredom becomes to spend money on things (as in your mind spending = enjoyment).

Why Are You Doing It?

To help you make it enjoyable, you should focus on the 'why'. That means, you need to establish a goal, so that it becomes more concrete. And no, 'because I should' isn't good enough. It's too abstract and doesn't create any sort of emotional connection. You have to attach other emotions to your goal, such as want and desire. The best way to do that is to find something to save for.

So, are you saving to buy a new house? For a wedding? For your child to get to go to university?? Do you want to be a millionaire? These are all good and measurable goals.

For me the way I learned to save money was when I decided I wanted to go traveling for a year. Then, whenever I wanted to buy a coffee, go out drinking, or get a new gadget, I remembered that that was my plan and I realized that this purchase today was going to mean I was either going to have to wait longer before I could leave or have less money (and less fun) when I did. And that simple realization made it possible for me not get that coffee, or keep my phone that might be scratched but still worked, or skip a night on the town.

And once the spending habits were broken, it was a cinch to keep them at bay. So now I'm quite minimalistic in my living because I would rather spend my money on experiences rather than things (as the research shows they make us far happier).

Set Micro Goals

The next step after you've established an overarching goal is to build smaller milestones that you can set. When you have a target, be it to make a million dollars in ten years, or to pay off your mortgage in five, then you've got to work out what that means for you per month, per week and per day.

And once that is worked out you have a daily target for you to reach for. This again serves to bring saving from some abstract notion into a day to day affair, where you know if you're succeeding or not from one day to the next.

Learn to Record Everything

If you want to save money, then 'the money you have' can't be some nebulous concept. Instead, you've got to know what's coming in and what's going out. It's only in this way that you can start working out where you could be more efficient with the money you've got. Often we'll find that we can save 10 to 15% of our expenses just by paying more careful attention to what we're doing and being a little smarter about how we buy, without even needing to scrimp!

So say 'yes' when people offer you a receipt and write everything you've got into a spread sheet, so that you can track your expenditures. How much are those nights on the town costing you? Are you on the right telephone plan? How much are you spending on food that you just end up throwing away? These are all things that only become clear when you embrace a more rigorous recording regiment.

Embrace The Money Minute

Even better, work on installing a money minute into your daily routine. What do I mean with that? A money minute is where you create a fixed time slot in your day to check your bank account, your receipts and your expenses.

This is something to do for two important reasons. The first one is that you eliminate that horrible feeling at the bottom of your stomach, where you're all stressed out about what's going on financially (and as a result don't look for months on end). After all, not that much will change from day to day.

Secondly (and just as importantly) through this you'll end up connecting actions with their consequences. If you go out for lunch, you'll see how much you spent. If you buy new pants, you'll see the consequences in your bank account. And once those two things are more closely connected this nebulous concept of 'credit' will disappear with the numbers of things start hitting home.

Hold Yourself Accountable

You can take a break from many things in life, but one thing you cannot take a break from is saving. That doesn't mean that you can't occasionally spend a little more than you should. These things happen. But what you should not do is not care about spending for a day. You've got to be accountable.

This means understanding that the binge mindset, "Oh I've already exceeded my daily spending, what does it matter if I exceed it a little more?" Doesn't work. A dollar spent is a dollar spent, no matter how many dollars you spent beforehand or afterwards. They all hold the same value.

Chapter 2: Habits & Attitudes of Saving

Habits are fantastic things. After all, you only have so much mental energy and the last thing we want to do is use it all up brushing our teeth or taking out the garbage. That's why habits are so important. They don't require all of our attention and thereby leave more energy for doing the things that matter, like laughing, creating and finding meaning.

Their advantage is also their problem, of course. Because since they don't require focus they rarely rise into awareness which means that that bad habits can be very tricky things to get rid of. That doesn't mean it's impossible however.

One of the best ways to deal with bad habits is to not actually focus on getting rid of them. Instead the focus should be on replacing it with a good one. And so, find below a set of good financial habits for you to cultivate.

Spending Mantras

Spending mantras are a great idea. They're a bit like rules that you try to introduce into your life. For example, "If I write for two hours straight right out of the gate, then I get to take a bath instead of a shower" or, "I will only order pizza if I went to the gym three times this week." Though they might sound pretty straight forward, they can actually exercise a dramatic influence over your life.

The idea is that you use guilt as a tool to keep you on the straight and narrow.

So how do you use them? Find a habit that you're not happy with, like for example that you go clubbing three times a week. Then you create a mantra like, "I will only go out more than twice if I have no credit card debt." Then you write that rule up in big words somewhere where you can see it, like on a piece of paper that you stick on your wall or the wallpaper of your phone.

And then you work very hard indeed to keep to it. For this reason, don't pick mantras that you know you can never fulfil, because when you do that you'll just end up ignoring it. Instead, aim for something that is actually achievable and that you can succeed at.

Share Your Ideas

Also, tell people about your mantras (as well as your goals and ambitions). Research shows that if you tell somebody else about your plans you'll be 33% more likely to actually carry through with them. That's a big jump for a few words!

It probably has something to do with you not wanting to embarrass yourself by having to tell your friend that you didn't actually go through with it. So in effect you're using negative emotions to get your way. But what's wrong with that? Why should we only use positive emotions to get what we want? If we use negative emotions, then they're at least good for helping us achieve something positive!

Even better, have somebody else who is also trying to get through a problem and then get together frequently to talk about how you're doing and to share ideas about how you can do better. This will make it a social occasion and even a little bit of a competition, adding a fun element into the entire exercise as you turn your attempts at self-improvement into an opportunity to socialize and bond with somebody.

Now, be careful about who you select. Don't choose somebody who will ultimately only enable your bad behavior. With that I mean somebody who is not invested in making you improve yourself, or somebody who has a vested interest in having you fail, be it to make themselves feel better, or because they want you to go out and splurge with (or on) them.

Don't Watch TV

Television is a consumerism machine with the occasional bit of plot over top. The entire television model is based on trying to get you to buy products, either through advertising or through product placement within the shows. These just make you want stuff and feel less good about yourself when you don't have them.

For example, research has shown that children who watch TV eat more food overall than children that don't – now unless you believe that's because television watching is tiring business, the advertising is going to have something to with that!

And besides, not consuming as much TV means you've got more time for other things, like a side business, developing skills and knowledge or hanging out with your family. Oh yes, and it saves on the electric bills, so really it's winning all around.

Automate Your Savings

Here's an idea, instead of relying on yourself to put money away get your bank to do it for you. We all have a credit account and most of us have a saving account. Now all you need to is get your bank to automatically send money from one to the other.

Even if it's just a few percent per month, it's already going to make a difference. Can't miss that percent right now? Then set it up immediately after you get a raise (or, if you know when you're going to get a raise in advance, set it up now to happen then – that's possible in quite a few bank accounts nowadays). Take half the raise for daily spending and get the other half put into a savings account. If you can do that every time you get a salary bump, you'll never feel the pain and your savings will increase ever more rapidly!

What's more, if you combine this with regularly checking your savings account, you'll very quickly start getting addicted to watching that little number grow to one of your preset goals (you have set goals, haven't you?) It will be like a game, where you're going for a high score – except that in this case the score remains when you close down your laptop and it has real world consequences!

Reject The Throw-Away Mindset

Do you really need a new phone? Is the one you're using today really that bad? Yes, I know that getting a new phone will make you look cool – but how useful is that if you're so poor that you're only eating porridge every day?

If every time you want to replace something you manage to put it off for a few months, you'll end up saving heaps of money. What's more, when you do get around to buying it, you'll feel far prouder of yourself and the purchase will feel like a reward for good behavior rather than just another purchase.

Also, see about repairing things that are only a little bit broken. This isn't just good for your budget (and it really is incredibly good for that) but it's also great for the environment. That's killing two birds with one stone, that is.

Freeze Your Credit Card

With this one I don't mean that you contact your bank and ask them to suspend your credit card. That's not half as fun as what I'm talking about. What I'm talking about is taking a bowl of water, putting your credit card inside and then putting it in the freezer. If you do this gently it won't damage your credit card. And it will be awesome to say you put your credit card on ice. It will make you feel like a mafia hit man.

More importantly, if you want to buy something, you'll have to thaw your credit card, which means you'll have to take it out of the fridge, wait for the ice to melt and then you can finally go out and use it. This means that you'll have the entire time while you wait for it to be ready to use for you to re-think your purchasing decision.

You can even turn it into a game. How long has your credit card been on ice? Hang a calendar on the fridge and mark off every week that you don't use it. Then you can count how many weeks you've been living within your means simply by looking at the Xs on your fridge door. How long do you think you can last?

Just Because It's Cheap Doesn't Mean It's a Good Deal

People love sales. They shouldn't. They're often very expensive – especially if you end up buying something that you don't really need. The lesson here is very simple. If you don't need it, it doesn't matter how much the discount is, it still means you're spending money you otherwise would still have had.

That's a bad deal for everybody except for the company selling you that crap.

So, unless you're going into the shop because you need something specific, don't let yourself be pulled in the door! I know it feels counterintuitive, but doing so will save you a great deal of money and will reduce how much regret you experience.

Do have to go buy something? Then go with somebody who hates shopping. The chance that you'll hang around in the shop looking at this, that or the other is much smaller when you're out with somebody who clearly doesn't want to be there.

Your partner hates to shop? Great! On the way to the restaurant stop by the shop to quickly pick up whatever you need. Explain to them why you're doing it with them tagging along. Then they can keep you on the straight and narrow.

We're Only Human

Screwed up? Bought something you shouldn't have? Spent too much money in the bar? It happens to the best of us. Forgive yourself. Treat it as a one-time mistake and move on. Don't agonize over it. I mean, kick yourself, but once is enough. The money is not going to come back, so hating yourself for it won't make things better.

Also, don't give up on saving because you screwed up. Saving is a journey and on every journey you can trip, slip or fall. And, yes, it really hurts when you do. The trick, however, is to get back up again and keep on walking down that road. That's the only way you'll be certain that you'll get where you're supposed to. So pick yourself up. You deserve it.

Chapter 3: Budgeting & Saving

Know What's Coming In

The first step to knowing how much you can spend is knowing how much is coming in. If you've got a basic salary per month this is a pretty straightforward calculation. The only thing that you do need to pay attention to is that you take your income after taxes, rather than before. What the government takes, you can't also spend.

If you collect wages per hour, then you're going to have to multiply what you bring in by the number of hours you work. Do not use the maximum hours that you'll work, as obviously you won't always work this many hours. Far better is to work from an income of the minimum hours you work. In that case, if you work more you can put that more into your savings account!

Don't have steady work? Then take your entire income over the last six to 12 months and divide that by six or twelve respectively to get a general idea. Here's an important thing to note with odd-job budgets. If you've got a good month don't think you can blow the extra money that has come in! You'll need that money to cover yourself when you've got a bad month (which will happen if this is the kind of work you do). So, whatever you do, resist the urge!

Next, add in any extra sources of income per month, like alimony, to that amount to get what you've got to work with. Do not add in bonus money, like a 13th month, overtime or anything like that. This is because there are often emergencies that push you over your budget and this money will help cushion those blows when they do hit. Don't have any bad luck? Great! Then you've got a bit of extra money to treat yourself or – better yet – put in your savings account!

Now doesn't that sound like a much more appealing situation than counting on that money as a part of your budget and then finding yourself in debt because you had some unexpected expense?

The Budget

Next, you can start working out your budget. The first step is to work out your fixed costs. Examples of these are your rent or mortgage and your debt payments. This also includes your insurance costs. Really, any money that you've got to pay every month that's fixed and unchanging goes into this category.

If you pay a yearly fee for something, like utilities, then divide that by 12 and putting that money aside each month for these costs. It's perfectly alright to park this money you in your savings account, where it can collect interest, and then to take it out again when the payment is due. Of course, in that case you still have to include it in your budget write-up. It is a monthly expense.

Next it's time to find out how much you're paying for groceries. If you've been collecting your receipts, then add them together and divide by the number of months your receipts span. Next check your bank statements to see how much you're withdrawing from the bank, then work out which percentage of that is necessities and which is wants (if you've kept receipts then that will be easy, if you haven't, you'll have to make a guestimate).

Add the necessities into your budget as well. Don't count your groceries double! If you pay for these with cash, then you can subtract them from this expenditure. Finally, take special expenses (like gifts, car maintenance, holidays, etc.) for the year, divide these by 12 and add them in there as well.

Congratulations, you've got your monthly budget! That's how much is going out at *a minimum* each month. I hope it's below what's coming in. The difference between income and outgoing is what's called disposable income. This is what you use for clothes, gadgets, big ticket items, school supplies, fun and savings. It's probably not as big as you thought, is it? Yes, that is unfortunate, but it's better than you know as budgeting by wishful thinking is not a viable alternative.

Emergency Funds

You never know when things are going to go wrong. For this reason, it's always a good idea to have an emergency fund available with cash that is readily accessible. This could be a credit card, or a shoebox under your bed, if that's what you prefer. What's important, however, that it's only ever used for emergencies. To help in that regard whenever you do have to use the fund immediately start topping up from your disposable income until it's back at the level that it's supposed to be.

When you're trying to bring your emergency fund up to a sizable level again, do not dip into your savings! Only do that if you've got some other emergency. Instead, forgo small pleasures as much as possible until the fund is back at the level it's supposed to be.

Shop Around for Discounts

The internet is a wonderful source of information about where you can get things more cheaply. If you're going to buy anything, then make sure you're aware where you might be able to get it more cheaply before you leave the house. This can save you a lot of money.

And don't just do this for big ticket items, either. If you're frequently buying smaller items (let's say tea bags) a few cents can quickly amount to a large amount of money.

For example, if you save $50 on a fridge, that sounds worthwhile, while if you save 2 cents on a teabag, that sounds like nothing major. If, however, your family goes through 7 bags a day, saving those 2 cents per bag will save you more in a year than you saved on the fridge! (51.10 dollars, in fact). And let's be clear about it, you only buy one fridge ever five to ten years or so – so imagine how much you'd save in that time on two cents per teabag? In this way small amounts can add up to a big difference!

Reduce Food and Drink Expenses

In a similar way, if you could save $2 a day taking food from home rather than buying food in town for your work, you'll save $10 a week a regular work week. Doesn't sound like much? It adds up to half a thousand dollars per year, you know. That comes to 26,000 dollars over a 50-year period. And that's if you put it under your couch, instead of investing it (in which case it would have been far more).

So whenever you want to buy something in town, perhaps think again. And if you really want to, then are you sure you need the biggest? If you take a smaller size (or a less luxurious sandwich) that can already make a huge difference. So don't go for the super mocha latte with cream and a shot of syrup. Take the filtered coffee instead. It will save you thousands of dollars in the long run!

Another good trick is if you have space for one of those big chest freezers is to get one of those. Then you can go out of your way to buy things you'll be certain to use a lot of in bulk. That can save you a great deal of money, as often buying in bulk can save you 10 or 20%. Even better, get one of those wholesaler cards, find out what goods won't spoil for at least a month and figure out how much of those you use on average, then drive down there and pick all that stuff up.

What do you use a lot of per month? Take all your grocery receipts and figure it out! Those receipts are more useful than you thought they were, aren't they?

And, of course, then there's inviting people over to your house instead of having dinner out on the town. Even if they don't pay anything towards the bill and don't bring a bottle of wine, you'll still be saving money as most restaurants charge you more than double of what you'd be paying if you would be eating at home. What's more, good friends will return the favor, which will mean you've got a free meal coming somewhere down the line!

Cutting Utilities Expenses

Going green isn't just good for the environment. It's good for your budget as well! LED lightbulbs and halogen bulbs will earn themselves back in a matter of months. In fact, the government agency Energy.gov says that just replacing the five most used lightbulbs with energy efficient ones will save you $75 in a year.

Double glazing your windows if you live in a place that either gets hot or cold can similarly make a big difference to your costs. Yes, these are big one-time costs, but will ultimately significantly cut your life-time spending on heating or air-conditioning and is therefore well worth considering.

Cutting Down On Vehicle Expenses

Getting a fuel efficient car, which isn't too big, will obviously make a huge difference to your bills. Of course, buying a new car might not be in your budget right now. What other things can you do to save money on your car?

First of all, wait and pray is not a good maintenance schedule. Yes, it sucks to go to the garage when you've got little money, but if you go early enough with small problems then they can be solved before they become big expensive problems.

What's more, if you go on time you still have a choice and can find a mechanic who is cheaper and schedule the fix for a time when you can do without the car or borrow somebody else's. Wait until the last minute, however, and all that is rendered impossible. So deal with problems in a timely manner!

To save fuel considered these strategies:
- **Take fewer trips.** Your car uses more fuel when the engine is cold. So if possible try to combine all your errands into one block rather than scattered over the day.
- **Don't drive in rush hour.** The stopping and starting makes you burn through way more fuel (and wastes your time besides).
- **When driving fast close the windows.** These create drag, which reduces fuel efficiency.
- **Remove external drag.** If you've got a roof rack or a ski box, or anything like that on the outside of the car, get rid of it! This causes more wind resistance and that increases your gas bill!
- **Clear the trunk.** Especially if you've got heavy stuff in the back, take it out. More weight means more fuel.
- **Don't jam the gas.** Driving like a racer (i.e. hard acceleration and hard brakes) costs you fuel. Instead, accelerate smoothly and let your car roll out as you approach a traffic light. This makes a big difference.
- **Air conditioners are fuel burners.** Really, they are. Don't use them when you don't need to.

- **Speed costs fuel.** The amount of fuel you need to push through the air as you accelerate is not a straight relationship. Instead it's squared. What that means is that every mile you try to go faster costs you significantly more fuel. So keep to the speed limit.
- **Flat tires drain fuel.** Keep your tires up to pressure as soft tires have more road surface and therefore create more drag. How much does adding a bit of air to your tires save? It saves you 4%. Doesn't sound like much? It's more than you imagine, after all most of us spend 2000 dollars a year on fuel, that means you'd save 80 bucks! Why wouldn't you do that since air is readily available at most gas stations?
- **Drive behind people.** Why push through the air when somebody ahead of you is already doing it? Staying behind other cars which are driving the same speed as you will make your trip consume considerably less fuel.

Also, remember that the foot wagon and the bike are great alternatives. The only fuel they use is your own and most of us can lose a few calories. Besides, both have been shown to improve both physical and mental health, which means less visits to the doctor and the psychologist.

Chapter 4: Spending

You know the saying: A dollar saved is a dollar earned.

Well, it is absolutely true. It doesn't matter where a dollar comes from, whether it be your boss or from not spending it on something else. It's still a dollar and can still be spent on the same things. In fact, especially in the beginning when you just start out in your quest to cut your spending, saving a dollar can be a far easier thing to accomplish then earning it.

And that matters. Because, let's face it. More than half of us do not like our jobs. That means the last thing we want to do is spend more time at our job in order to earn more money. So, spending less is a far more attractive way to find the extra dollars that you can put away.

For that reason, here we're going to look at ways to cut your spending, so that you don't have to work longer hours or find a better-paying job (though you can still do so if you like).

Don't Try to Keep Up with The 'Joneses'

A lot of us mistake status for happiness. With this I mean that we believe that if more people will like us or be impressed with us we'll like or be impressed by ourselves. And, since the main way we demonstrate status is by buying it, we therefore end up spending money impressing others.

For example, we might move into a bigger house, replace last year's phone with this year's or buy expensive cars, even though objectively the things we had were largely fine.

Leaving aside, for the moment, that there is very little scientific evidence to support that we actually end up happier as a result of having more status, it is a very expensive we to pursue happiness. You see, to get status you don't just need more expensive things, you need to have more expensive things than the people you comparing yourself to.

And as they're out there buying stuff as well, it becomes a competition.

This is called a zero sum game, which means that whenever one person wins another person has to lose. In other words, if I buy a new Rolex, the people around me look worse off than me in comparison. Then, when they compensate by buying something equally or even more expensive, then *my* status drops.

In other words, if the people around you match your status spending increases, then everybody's status will remain the same even while we spend more and more. It is, in other words, a status-based arms race.

Therefore, if you're struggling financially, choose to opt out of this race – at least for a while. Save the money that instead. Then use that to not just change your situation incrementally but drastically. For example, by getting a better education, by getting rid of debt, or by getting all your ducks in a row so that you can find a better job. If you can pull that off then you won't just get a leg up in the race, you can change it entirely.

Though be aware, there are always new people to compete against.

Know The Difference Between 'Needs' and 'Wants'

This is vital. If you spend all your money on wants, then you won't have what you need, namely money tucked away to start that business idea you've got, to move into a neighborhood where your kids can go to a great school, or to pay for the medical emergency that might come along.

When is something a need and when is something a want? You need something if not having it will give you medical problems, a shorter lifespan, or will get you arrested. So you need food, you need to keep warm and you need to pay your outstanding traffic fines. You do not need a new pair of shoes if you've already got several, you do not need chocolate ice cream and you do not need to drink on a Friday.

Yes, it might feel like it after a long hard week, but that doesn't make it true.

This is not to say that you can't indulge your wants. Instead, what I'm saying is that you need understand that that is what you're doing when you do, so that you can consider whether you'd rather spend that money now or would rather have that money for something else down the line.

You can only spend the dollar once. So make certain you're spending it on what you really want to.

You Are Worth It

Yes, you might be worth that nice puppy in the window. You might be worth that nice tie you saw in the rack. You might even be worth a night out dancing. But aren't you also worth your dreams? I don't know what yours are, but I know that every dream costs money. And if you're not saving you're not bringing those dreams any closer to becoming a reality.

So every time you're planning on spending money on a want take a moment to think to yourself, "Is it worthy of me? Is it worthy of delaying my dream of starting my life as a painter, being free of university debt, writing my first novel, or starting my own business?" Only if you can answer that in the affirmative should you buy it.

The best way to make sure you've thought things through sufficiently is by installing a 30-day rule. This is very simple. Postpone any want-based purchase by 30 days. If you still want it after that, then you know it's not just you seeking instant gratification. What's more, by doing this, when you do buy something it will be a reward for having such patience, rather than you satisfying some ill-considered urge, and that will make it all the more enjoyable.

Don't Buy Off Your Kids but Spend Time with Them

Sometimes you want to take the kids to Disneyland, but most of the time, just planting a garden, playing catch, or going to look at the ducks in the pond will be enough. Kids, especially young ones, just want to have time with you and it doesn't really matter where they do so.

So, instead of buying them off with toys, spend time with them building your own cool stuff from a couple of empty egg cartons, some toilet paper rolls and a bunch of crayons. They'll often treasure those memories far more than any toy you may want to buy them.

Chapter 5: Debt, Credit Cards & Interest

Pay Off Debt Before You Start Saving

Want to save? If you've got debt, pay it off first. This might not feel as satisfying as saving money, but it will make you hundreds, if not thousands, of dollars a year. Let's take a worst case scenario. Let's say you've got credit card debt.

You see, the average credit card rate right now is 15% per year. That means that every dollar you've got in debt will grow by 15 cents if you don't pay it this year. Leave that for another year and you've got a debt of $1.32 per original dollar. That means if you don't do anything about your debt it will double in 5 years.

"But if I'm paying off my credit card debt then I'm not saving", some of you may cry. And a lot of people feel that way. But that argument makes no sense. If you're paying off your credit card and you desperately need the money, then you can always go back to your credit card. That's not the same, you say. And no, it isn't.

It's a far smarter strategy.

Let's do some simple math. You've got $2000 in debt and manage to save 2000 dollars. In one scenario you save the money. In the other scenario you pay off your debt. What does this mean for the two scenarios?

- The credit card makes you pay an extra 15%, so your debt there is $2300. Your savings makes you 3%, so there you've got $2060. Leaving you with 2060 (savings) − 2300 (credit card debt) = -240
- In the other situation you pay off the credit card debt and do not pay interest or collect interest. So here it's 0.
- That means that the first situation is more than 10% as bad as situation two.

So which situation would you rather be in?

Compound Interest

Much like credit card debt is a real drag, having your money in a proper savings account with a decent rate of return is something you should aim to do as quickly as possible. Here it's vital to shop around for a place that gives you the best return imaginable. Even a one percent difference can make you a huge amount of money.

For example, if you get a measly 2% interest it will take you 35 years to double your money, while if it's 3 that some money will double in value in 23.5 years. Found a place that pays you 5%? Then it will double in about 14 years, meaning that in 28 years' time that money will have doubled and then doubled again, so that a thousand would have become four thousand. And you don't have to do anything for that. That's free money. Sound pretty good, right?

How to Deal with Major Debt

Okay, but what if you're not there yet? What if you're one of those people still trying to fight their way through a big pile of debt? Here are some ideas to consider.

- **Sell of the stuff you don't really need.**
  Have a baseball card collection, a bunch of
  video games, or a car that you don't use, or an
  attic full of stuff that's really just collecting
  dust? Sell all of it and throw that money at the
  debt, preferably the one with the highest
  interest rate (usually your credit card debt). By
  reducing this debt, you'll end up paying less
  money in interest payments, which will mean
  that more of the money you pay towards your
  debt goes towards actually paying your debt
  (which in turn will mean even less interest the
  next time you pay, thereby creating a virtuous
  cycle!).

- **Don't set your sights on the whole
  mountain.** Instead, focus on getting rid of a
  manageable portion. Every time you do that,
  you'll feel better, have to pay less interest and
  be closer to your goal of getting rid of it all.

- **Save hard.** Try to go *truly* frugal for a few
  months and throw everything at getting rid of
  your highest-interest debt. Now don't think that
  you've got to do this the whole time, just for a
  few months. The goal here is to make a sizable
  dent – once again, with the goal of getting some
  of that interest payment under control.

Also, try to restructure that debt to lower interest rates. If you've got some sort of equity, then borrow against that and use that money to pay off the high rate debt, particularly what you have in credit cards (and then cut them up so that you don't end up doubling your debt!) This can often drastically reduce your interest payments.

Alternatively talk with credit cards about hardship programs. These can last from a few months to a long time, where you pay less interest and get other sorts of help to get you back on the straight and the narrow. Now, they don't advertise these as they hurt their bottom line, but they're willing to consider if you're eligible if they believe that putting you on a program will make it more likely that you'll pay back your debt then if you don't. (They'd rather have some money than none at all).

For that reason, it's important that your credit history is in good order. So approach both the bank and the credit card companies before things go pear shaped, if possible. Admittedly, it might be uncomfortable to have to show your financial situation as well have people scrutinize your spending. At the same time, if that means you'll have to spend thousands less on interest payments (And means you can be out of debt years earlier) it is worth it.

Chapter 6: Housing

Live More Cheaply

Are you renting a place that is really too big for what you need? Is your house a constant nightmare of costs and maintenance? Then get out! There is no reason that you can't move into something more suitable for yourself and your family. And remember, just because you're downgrading now doesn't mean you're downgrading your life. You can upgrade again when things go better – which they will far more quickly if you're spending a few hundred dollars less on rent and maintenance.

There is no shame in downgrading your house. It's a smart investment of the limited resources you have (and remember, all of our resources are limited). This way, you can have more money to go on holiday, more money to save up for a place to buy, or more money to get that education you always wanted.

And what's more important, what other people might think or your own future?

To Rent or Buy

It really depends on one question: can you consistently pay your mortgage? After all, as long as you've got a mortgage you don't actually own your house (even if people say you do). It's the bank that owns it. It's only once you've paid it all of that that changes. Of course, at that point you'll own a piece of property and that's absolutely wonderful – and can be a serious asset to you and later your children.

The thing is, can you actually wait that long? Is it worth it for you to get stuck with a house, or would you rather have the possibility to move? After all, if you're renting, then if the area you're living in becomes economically depressed, you've got the possibility to move somewhere where the getting is good. That's not possible if you're stuck with a house that you can't sell. In that case it can become a real ball and chain.

Buying a house is like willingly going into a long tunnel with a very bright light at the end. If you can make it to the other side of that tunnel, you're golden. Still, you're going to be underground for a long time and committed to staying the course while you are.

Conclusion

And that almost brings us to the end. I hope you've found some useful tips in this book to help you make the right decisions towards saving money. If nothing else, make sure you remember that saving isn't about not spending, it's about so much more than that.

It's a mindset. It's a way of looking at the world. It's a realization that your whole life hangs together and what you do today affects what you do tomorrow, the day after and every day after that – much like compound interest.

Some people say that we should live every day as if it's our last. But if that were true, who would go to work, who would bother brushing their teeth and why not just stay out all night blowing through your money? Yes, you shouldn't live your life in a constant quest to avoid tomorrow's regret. That will make for a boring life indeed, but you can't just pretend there is no tomorrow, next week, or next year.

Life is a journey. And only you get to choose if it's towards some better place, or towards somewhere dark and unpleasant. If you consistently sacrifice later at the shrine of now, then eventually there will be nothing but misery on the horizon.

And that while saving doesn't even have to be a chore! It can be an adventure all on its own, where you aim to make your situation better by making yourself better. And that can become its own reward. It can even lead to greater things, as you take the discipline that you've managed to work up saving into other pursuits – be it art, learning or your job.

Truth be told, hedonism and seeking out simple pleasure get old sooner than you think. The only thing that stays pleasurable is a constant journey of self-actualization and improvement. And learning how to save might just be the first step down that path.

So good luck and good saving!

Inspirational Quotes on Money

(A Selection of Some of the Best Quotes About Money)

"Beware of little expenses; a small leak will sink a great ship."
~ Benjamin Franklin ~

"Someone's sitting in the shade today because someone planted a tree a long time ago."
~ Warren Buffett ~

"A budget is telling your money where to go, instead of wondering where it went."
~ John C. Maxwell ~

"The person who doesn't know where his next dollar is coming from usually doesn't know where his last dollar went."
        ~ Unknown ~

"Wealth gained hastily will dwindle, but whoever gathers little by little will increase it."
        ~ Proverbs 13:11 ~

"If we fasten our attention on what we have, rather than what we lack, a very little wealth is sufficient."
        ~ Francis Johnson ~

"The urge to spend all you make is called consumer mentality. Try to get investment mentality instead."
        ~ Edward H. Romney ~

"Financial peace isn't the acquisition of stuff. It's learning to live on less than you make, so you can have money to invest. You can't win until you do this."
~ Dave Ramsey ~

"He who loses money, loses much; He who loses a friend, loses much more; He who loses faith, loses all."
~ Eleanor Roosevelt ~

"It's good to have money and the things money can buy, but it's good, too, to check up once in a while and make sure that you haven't lost the things that money can't buy."
~ George Horace Lorimer ~

"Money never made a man happy yet, nor will it. There is nothing in its nature to produce happiness. The more a man has, the more he wants. Instead of filling a vacuum, it makes one."
~ Benjamin Franklin ~

"You can only become truly accomplished at something you love. Don't make money your goal. Instead, pursue the things you love doing, and then do them so well that people can't take their eyes off you."
~ Maya Angelou ~

"Time is more valuable than money. You can get more money, but you cannot get more time."
~ Jim Rohn ~

"Empty pockets never held anyone back. Only empty heads and empty hearts can do that."
~ Norman Vincent Peale ~

"All hard work brings a profit, but mere talk leads only to poverty."
~ Proverbs 14:23 ~

"If your riches are yours, why don't you take them with you to the other world?"
    ~ Benjamin Franklin ~

"Many people take no care of their money till they come nearly to the end of it, and others do just the same with their time."
    ~ Johann Wolfgang von Goethe ~

"When you have money, think of the time when you had none."
    ~ Japanese Proverb ~

"When I had money everyone called me brother."
    ~ Polish proverb ~

"When it comes to money, you can't win. If you focus on making it, you're materialistic. If you try to but don't make any, you're a loser. If you make a lot and keep it, you're a miser. If you make it and spend it, you're a spendthrift. If you don't care about making it, you're unambitious. If you make a lot and still have it when you die, you're a fool--for trying to take it with you. The only way to really win with money is to hold it loosely--and be generous with it to accomplish things of value."

~ *John C. Maxwell* ~

Check Out Other Books

	Your Money or Your Life: 9 Steps to Transforming Your Relationship with Money and Achieving Financial Independence: Revised and Updated for the 21st Century ASIN: B0052MD8VO https://goo.gl/9ft2bG
	Why Didn't They Teach Me This in School? 99 Personal Money Management Principles to Live By ASIN: B00C5UM9MA https://goo.gl/6WTkWA
	How to Make Your Money Last: The Indispensable Retirement Guide ASIN: B00P434BTE https://goo.gl/umWpQL
	How to Save Money Without Really Trying: A Step-by-Step Guide to Saving $1,000 Per Month ASIN: B01C14210E https://goo.gl/3uTLtW